The Wonderful Names of Jesus

by Warren W. Wiersbe
Assistant Bible Teacher
Back to the Bible Broadcast

A
BACK TO THE BIBLE
PUBLICATION

Back to the Bible
Lincoln, Nebraska 68501

80,000 printed to date—1980
(5-9782—80M—120)
ISBN 0-8474-6501-2

Printed in the United States of America

Contents

Chapter 1

The Nazarene

I have not counted them, but a friend of mine claims that there are more than 700 different names and titles of Jesus Christ found in the Bible. Jesus Christ is so great in His person and work that it takes hundreds of names and titles to describe Him. Why should we study these names? For this reason: *Every name that He wears is a blessing that He shares.* The better we understand the names of our Lord Jesus Christ, the better we will know Him; and the better we know Him, the better we know what He has done for us and can do for us.

Understanding the Name

"And he came and dwelt in a city called Nazareth: that it might be fulfilled which was spoken by the prophets, He shall be called a Nazarene" (Matt. 2:23). Perhaps the most common name that was used to identify our Lord when He was here on earth was "Jesus of Nazareth," or "Jesus the Nazarene."

Jesus was born in Bethlehem of Judea, but the people did not identify Him with Bethlehem; they identified Him with Nazareth in Galilee. It was in Nazareth that He spent most of His earthly life. At the age of 30, when He began His ministry, Jesus left Nazareth and began to travel throughout the various parts of the Holy Land. Because He came from Nazareth, Jesus was given the title "Jesus of Nazareth."

According to Matthew, this was in fulfillment of prophecy—that "which was spoken by the prophets, He shall be called a Nazarene" (v. 23). The interesting thing is this: You can search the Old Testament, and you will not find Nazareth mentioned even once. Nazareth is mentioned several times in the New Testament, but not in the Old Testament. And nowhere in the Old Testament do we find a specific prophecy that says, "He shall be called a Nazarene." So we have two tasks before us: first, we must try to understand this name, and second, we must apply the name and see what it means to us personally.

Let's begin by trying to understand the name "Nazarene." Please do not confuse "Nazarene" with the title "Nazirite." In Numbers 6 are the specifications concerning the Nazirites. The word Nazirite means "one who is separated." To be sure, the Lord Jesus Christ was totally separated unto God. He was "holy, harmless, undefiled" (Heb. 7:26). But the Lord Jesus Christ was not a Nazirite. For example, Nazirites were not supposed to touch dead bodies, but Jesus did. Nazirites were not supposed to be identified with the fruit of the vine, but our Lord was. In contrast to John the Baptist (who was a Nazirite), the Lord Jesus Christ attended dinners, He went to wedding feasts, and He did not separate Himself from the everyday social life of the people. So the name "Nazarene" is not equivalent to "Nazirite," although our Lord Jesus was totally separated unto God.

Many Bible students associate the name "Nazarene" with the Hebrew word *netzer,* which means "a branch." In a number of Old Testament references, our Lord Jesus is associated with this title. For example, Jeremiah 23:5 says, "I will raise unto David a righteous Branch." In Zechariah 3:8 He is called "my servant the Branch." In Zechariah 6:12,13 He is called "the man whose name is The Branch." In Isaiah 4:2 He is called "the branch of the Lord." It looked as though David's family tree had been chopped down and that nothing was left. Then along came the Lord Jesus, born into David's family, "a root out of a dry ground" (Isa. 53:2). He is the "branch" who will continue David's reign and establish the kingdom.

We have a problem, however, if we connect "Nazarene" with the Hebrw word *netzer.* The four passages that refer to the Lord Jesus as the "branch" do not use the word *netzer;* they use another Hebrew word for "branch." Only in Isaiah 11:1 do we find a prophecy about the Lord Jesus using the word *netzer.*

I do not think that "Nazarene" comes from *netzer,* and it certainly does not come from the term "Nazirite." Then what does it come from? We must remember what Nazareth was in Jesus' day. When Philip was converted and went and called his friend

7

Nathanael to come and meet the Lord Jesus, Nathanael said, "Can any good thing come out of Nazareth?" (John 1:46). You see, back in that day Nazareth was a despised and rejected place. It had a mixed population of Jews and Gentiles; the people spoke a very rough dialect; some of the rebels of that day lived in Nazareth. Nazareth was, as we would say, "on the other side of town" or "on the other side of the tracks." And so when you called somebody a "Nazarene," you were saying he was not in the social register, he was not listed in the *Who's Who* of his day. I think our Lord Jesus was known as a Nazarene because He was "despised and rejected of men; a man of sorrows, and acquainted with grief" (Isa. 53:3). In the Old Testament several of the prophets—including Isaiah and Jeremiah—and the psalmists talked about the Lord Jesus Christ as the One who was rejected.

Applying His Name

Now let's apply the name to our own lives. What does it mean to you and to me today that Jesus Christ was called a Nazarene?

The Grace of God

For one thing, this name speaks to me about *the grace of God*. When Jesus Christ, the Son of God, came into history, He did not identify with Jerusalem, the great city of religion. He did not go to Rome, the great city of law. He did not go to Athens, the great city of philosophy. Where did He go? He went to Nazareth— He identified with the people who were despised and rejected, the poor and the needy. And yet the Lord Jesus took that name "Nazareth" and glorified it: "Jesus of Nazareth." Wouldn't you be happy to have your name identified with Jesus? Nazareth, despised by men, was glorified by Jesus Christ because He identified Himself with it. The sad thing is that people of Nazareth rejected Him. A prophet is always without honor in his own country among his own people (see Matt. 13:57).

The name "Nazareth" was lifted up to the cross. You will recall that Pilate had made a title and put it on the cross: "Jesus of Nazareth, the King of the Jews" (John 19:19). Can you imagine that—Nazareth put up on the cross! When the people came to the tomb after our Lord's resurrection, the angel said, "Ye seek Jesus of Nazareth" (Mark 16:6). Can you imagine angels mentioning Nazareth?

Our Lord Jesus Himself used the name "Nazareth" when He spoke from heaven. In Acts 22:8, at the conversion of the Apostle Paul, our Lord said, "I am Jesus of Nazareth." He took that name Nazareth and lifted it all the way up to heaven! Yet the sad thing is that the people of Nazareth rejected Him.

No matter where you live, no matter how much you own, no matter how important you may be to other people, Jesus Christ comes to where you are. He identifies Himself with those who are needy and

9

rejected. All during His earthly ministry, He identified with publicans and sinners, He identified with lepers and sick people—those who were not wanted, those who were outcasts. Jesus of Nazareth is still passing by, and by faith you can reach out and say, "Lord Jesus, save me; Lord Jesus, help me—this is my need today."

The Word of God

This name speaks to me not only of the grace of God but also of *the Word of God*. Do you know *why* the Lord Jesus lived in Nazareth? Because God's Word told Him to. At least 12 times in his Gospel Matthew said, "This was done that it might be fulfilled which was written by the prophet." Do you know why Jesus was born in Bethlehem? The prophet said He would be. Do you know why those babies were slain in Bethlehem? The prophet said it would happen. Do you know why He went to Nazareth? Because the prophets said He would be called a Nazarene—despised and rejected. You see, whatever Jesus did was in fulfillment of the Word of God.

That encourages me! If you and I will just simply obey the Word of God, we will live as Jesus lived. We should work where we work because God tells us to. We should do what we do because God tells us to. This name "Nazarene" magnifies the grace of God, and it magnifies the Word of God. Live according to what the Bible says. Obey God's Word.

10

There is a third lesson that comes from this name: We should be identified with *the sufferings of Christ*. Jesus came to a despised and rejected place. He Himself was despised and rejected, and we should share in His reproach. Hebrews 13:13 tells us we should go "without the camp, bearing his reproach." Don't be afraid to suffer for the Lord Jesus. Don't be ashamed to be identified with Him. He was not ashamed to be identified with us. In Acts 24:5 His enemies called the Christians "the sect of the Nazarenes." That was quite a title—"the sect of the Nazarenes"! They looked down upon the Christians. They said, "Who are these people identified with Jesus of Nazareth?"

Never be ashamed of the Lord Jesus. We are "not ashamed of the gospel of Christ; for it is the power of God unto salvation to every one that believeth" (Rom. 1:16). We are not to be ashamed to take up His cross and follow Him. In fact, we should be honored to be identified with Jesus Christ—Jesus of Nazareth, Jesus the Nazarene.

The grace of God, the Word of God and the sufferings of Christ—these are all wrapped up in this wonderful name, "Jesus the Nazarene." Let's live by the grace of God, and let's obey the Word of God, and let's be very, very careful that in everything we do we are not ashamed of the Lord Jesus Christ.

Perhaps you have never trusted Christ as your Saviour. I'd like to encourage you to trust Him.

11

Jesus comes to where you are to make you what you ought to be. Nathanael said, "Can any good thing come out of Nazareth?" (John 1:46). Yes, something good did come out of Nazareth—the Lord Jesus Christ, the holy Son of God. He left Nazareth and ministered to needy people. Wherever there was hurt, Jesus was there to heal. Where there was sin, He was there to forgive. If you will just open your heart and trust Christ as your Saviour, you will be saved by the grace of God. You can then live in obedience to the Word of God. You can then be identified with Him in "the fellowship of his sufferings" (Phil. 3:10), bearing His reproach, unashamed of the Lord Jesus Christ, and living to glorify Him.

"Jesus of Nazareth passeth by" (Luke 18:37). Will you trust Him now?

Chapter 2

The Pioneer

The Word of God tells us that Jesus Christ came to be a pioneer. If you read your Bible carefully, you may say, "Pastor Wiersbe, I have never seen the word 'pioneer' in my Bible." Well, it's there, but it is translated "prince." In Acts 5:31, when Peter was speaking to the council, he said, "Him [the Lord Jesus] hath God exalted with his right hand to be a Prince and a Saviour, and to give repentance to Israel, and forgiveness of sins."

The word "prince" is a Greek word that is made up of two other words which mean "to begin" and "to lead." The word "Prince" really means "someone who starts something, who opens up the way that others might follow." I really think the best translation (and many Greek students agree) is the word "pioneer."

There is something fascinating about the pioneer days. Many cities have "pioneer days" for celebrating their founding. We watch television programs about the pioneer days. There is something challenging, something fascinating about the pioneers. A man with his family goes off into new territory—he opens the way for others to follow. He is a trailblazer. That is the meaning of this word in Acts

5:31: "Him hath God exalted with his right hand to be a Prince"—to be a pioneer!

Three other references to this title of our Lord Jesus are found in the New Testament, and I want to share them with you. They open up for us three different aspects of our Lord's ministry. Every name that Jesus wears is a blessing that He shares.

Jesus is the Pioneer—He wants to lead us into new frontiers. The tragedy is that too many of us as Christians are standing still. Actually, we don't stand still in the Christian life; we either move forward or we go backward. I know the desire of your heart is to go forward in the Christian life. In your praying, in your ministering, in your understanding of the Word of God, in your giving, in all of the outreach of your life, your desire is to go forward and to make progress.

A pioneer has to move into new territory. Some of God's people don't like to move into new territory—they want to keep walking on the same treadmill. But if you want to make progress in your Christian life, then learn what it means to have Jesus Christ as your Pioneer.

Pioneer of Life

Our first reference is Acts 3:13-15. Once again Peter is speaking about the Lord Jesus: "The God of Abraham, and of Isaac, and of Jacob, the God of our fathers, hath glorified his Son Jesus; whom ye delivered up, and denied in the presence of Pilate, when he was determined to let him go. But ye

14

denied the Holy One and the Just, and desired a murderer to be granted unto you; and killed the Prince of life, whom God hath raised from the dead, of which we are witnesses." Let me restate what Peter said: "And killed the [Pioneer] of life" (v. 15). That is quite a statement about our Lord Jesus— He is the Pioneer of life.

Too many people are concerned about making a living, but they are not concerned about making a life. They know the price of everything but the value of nothing. They are merely existing and just drifting. Along comes the Lord Jesus who says, "Look, I am the Pioneer of life! I want you to walk on this road that leads to life everlasting. I have opened a new and a living way, and I want you to share in it." He is the Pioneer of life.

There is quite a paradox in this statement: "[You] killed the Prince of life." How could you kill the Prince of life? As God, Jesus is the eternal one, but as man, He could die for us. Had He not died, there could be no life for lost sinners. It's a paradox, I know. He who is the Prince of life had to die to open the way of life for us. Jesus said, "I am the way, the truth, and the life" (John 14:6). If you put all of that together, it would read: "I am the true and the living way. I am the way that you can trust. I am the way that gives you life." He is the Pioneer of life.

I think the word "life" is perhaps the best description of what it means to be a Christian. "He that hath the Son hath life" (I John 5:12). When you trust Christ as your Saviour, you receive *eternal* life. And

15

you receive *abundant* life as you follow the Pioneer of life wherever He leads you.

This is illustrated so beautifully in Acts 3. Peter and John went to prayer meeting at the temple, and they met a lame man—a man who had been lame from birth; he had never walked. And he was a beggar. Friends carried him to the Beautiful Gate of the temple, and there he would beg alms from the people going into the temple services. He saw Peter and John and expected to get something from them. Peter said to him, "Silver and gold have I none; but such as I have give I thee; in the name of Jesus Christ of Nazareth, rise up and walk" (v. 6). Peter reached out, took him by the right hand and lifted him up; and the man was instantly healed.

Up to that point, this man had not had much life. He was born a cripple. You and I, spiritually speaking, were born "cripples." When we were born the first time, we were born crippled because of sin. We were born beggars—we had nothing of ourselves. We brought nothing into this world, and we are going to take nothing out of this world. This man was a cripple, he could not help himself. This crippled beggar could never blaze any pioneer trails. Then along came the apostles who introduced him to Jesus. The Lord Jesus Christ became to this man the Pioneer of life. The man stood up! He began to leap and walk! He entered into the temple with the disciples, "walking, and leaping, and praising God" (v. 8). Yes, the Lord Jesus Christ is the Pioneer of life.

Has Jesus opened the way of life for you? Have

you trusted Him as your Saviour, and are you following Him as your Lord? If you are, then you are moving forward on that road of life. Psalm 16:11 says, "Thou wilt shew me the path of life." The Lord Jesus Christ opened the way of life that you and I might follow. He is the Pioneer of life.

Pioneer of Salvation

There is a second reference we must look at—Hebrews 2:10. The Book of Hebrews was written to a group of Jewish believers to encourage them to go forward in their Christian life. These believers were tempted by what they could see—they could see the temple, the sacrifices, the city of Jerusalem, the priests and all the temple services. But they had been saved, and they were living by the invisible. They had a High Priest in heaven, but they could not see Him. They had a city in heaven, but they could not see it. For them there were no more sacrifices; there was no more priesthood on earth. These Jewish believers were tempted to go back to the visible and not walk by faith in the invisible.

In Hebrews 2:10 we read this: "For it became him [God the Father], for whom are all things, and by whom are all things, in bringing many sons unto glory, to make the captain of their salvation perfect through sufferings." Now the "Captain of our salvation" is the Lord Jesus Christ. That word "captain" is the word "pioneer." He is the Pioneer of salvation.

This truth excites me! Many people think salvation is a static experience. They say, "I've trusted Jesus Christ. I've been born again, and that's it!" But salvation involves so much more than just the forgiveness of sins and being born into the family of God! The Lord Jesus Christ is the Pioneer of our salvation. This means there is always something more to learn! There is always something new to experience in this wonderful thing called salvation.

Just think for a moment about the people in Jerusalem who went to the temple and took part in all the ceremonies. They were limited in their progress. For example, when they came to the temple, they could only go as far as the altar. They could not go back into the Holy Place. The Levites and the priests could go into the Holy Place of the temple, but even they could not go into the Holy of Holies. Only the high priest could go into the Holy of Holies, and he did that once a year on the Day of Atonement. For those Jewish people, there was always a barrier—something stood in the way. But for those who are Christians, nothing stands in the way. That is why Hebrews 10:19,20 encourages us to come boldly into the Holy of Holies by a new and living way which Jesus Christ consecrated for us.

The question I want to ask is this: Is your salvation experience static and boring? Are you standing still or going backward? Then follow the Pioneer of your salvation! As you follow Him, salvation becomes a growing and a glowing experience. As you follow Him, He takes you through the veil and into the very Holy of Holies.

Pioneer of Faith

Our third reference, Hebrews 12:2, says, "Looking unto Jesus, the author and finisher of our faith." He is not only the Pioneer of life and the Pioneer of salvation, but He is also the Pioneer of faith. Do you know what that means? That means that our faith has to make progress. We cannot stand still. Faith must grow. The Bible mentions "no faith," "little faith," "faith" and "great faith." I wonder what kind of report card I would get if God were to grade me on my faith? Jesus Christ is the Pioneer of our faith. He is the "author and finisher of our faith." As the Pioneer, whatever He starts, He finishes. That is the beautiful thing about following the Lord Jesus. When you trust His Word, you know He will finish what He starts.

Many people today are hurting; perhaps you are among them. You have problems—you are wondering why God has permitted certain things to happen to you. Here is the wonderful news: The Pioneer, the Lord Jesus, wants you to grow. He wants you to make progress in your Christian life. He wants you to move forward. He wants to give you new experiences of blessing and enrichment. He's the Pioneer of life—He will guide your path. He is the Pioneer of salvation—there will always be new experiences of joy and blessing and growth. He is the Pioneer of faith—He wants you to grow in your faith and to become stronger.

How do we follow the Pioneer of our salvation? Through the Word. God has spoken to us through

19

His Word, and it is important that you and I study the Word, obey the Word and trust the Word. Did you read your Bible today? Did you pray today? Whatever your burden or problem may be, take time to get alone with the Pioneer of life, the Pioneer of salvation, the Pioneer of faith. If you follow Him, you will start to move forward in an exciting new way in your Christian life and testimony.

Chapter 3

The Carpenter

When our Lord was teaching here on earth, He talked about many different vocations. He said one day, "Behold, a sower went forth to sow" (Matt. 13:3). But Jesus was not a farmer when He was on earth. He said, "I am the good shepherd" (John 10:14). But when He was here on earth, our Lord was not a shepherd. Do you know what He was? He was a carpenter.

"And he went out from thence, and came into his own country [Nazareth]; and his disciples follow him. And when the sabbath day was come, he began to teach in the synagogue: and many hearing him were astonished, saying, From whence hath this man these things? and what wisdom is this which is given unto him, that even such mighty works are wrought by his hands? Is not this the carpenter, the son of Mary, the brother of James, and Joses, and of Juda, and Simon? and are not his sisters here with us? And they were offended at him. But Jesus said unto them, A prophet is not without honour, but in his own country, and among his own kin, and in his own house. And he could there do no mighty work, save [except] that he laid his hands upon a few sick folk, and healed them. And he marvelled because of their unbelief. And he went round about the villages, teaching" (Mark 6:1-6).

Why was it, when Jesus came to earth, He chose the vocation of carpenter? He was a teacher, and He was a healer, but He taught and healed after He had been a carpenter. During the years that He lived in Nazareth, He worked at a bench as a carpenter.

A Carpenter's Home

Let me suggest several reasons why our Lord was a carpenter. First of all, He was born into a carpenter's home. Joseph, His earthly father, was a carpenter. In Matthew 13:55 we read, "Is not this the carpenter's son?" The Lord Jesus was born into a carpenter's home. This was not what the Jewish people expected at all. They thought that their Messiah would come as a great king and would be born in a palace. But He was born into a carpenter's home. He should have been born a great soldier, a conqueror, who would deliver them from Rome. No, He came as a laborer, He came as a servant—a carpenter.

The Old Testament Scriptures predicted that He would come as a servant. In Isaiah 52 and 53 is a description of the suffering servant of the Lord. In Philippians 2:5-8 we are told that Jesus Christ came as a servant. When our Lord Jesus Christ came into this world, according to Hebrews 10:7, He said, "I come . . . to do thy will, O God." Jesus came as a humble servant; He came as a carpenter.

The Lord Jesus Christ identified Himself with

common people. We read in the Scriptures that the common people heard Him gladly, because He knew what they were like and He knew what they needed. He knew the dignity of honest labor, He knew what it was like to work, to be tired. The Jewish people have many sayings; one is this: "If you do not teach your son how to work, you teach him how to be a thief." All of the Jewish people taught their sons how to work. Even the rabbis had their vocation, their work. Paul, you will recall, was a tentmaker. Jesus was a carpenter. That says to me that when Jesus Christ came to this earth He identified with all of us.

A Carpenter's Work

There is a second reason why I think our Lord became a carpenter when He was here on earth. Not only was He born into a carpenter's home, but also He came to do a carpenter's work. What does a carpenter do? He builds and he repairs. I must admit to you that I do not have that kind of skill. How I wish I could take tools and go around our house and fix things, but I simply do not have those skills. Other members of my family do, but not I. The Lord Jesus Christ was skilled at building and repairing. He came to do a carpenter's work.

I can just imagine people coming to the carpenter shop there in Nazareth and bringing Jesus broken tables and chairs or giving Him orders for new pieces of furniture or farm equipment. Jesus spent those years building and repairing.

Before He came to earth, He had built the universe. He knew something about building. "All things were made by him; and without him was not any thing made that was made" (John 1:3). He built the universe.

Today the Lord Jesus Christ is building His Church (Matt. 16:18). The Church is not some denomination or some man-made organization. The Church is made up of all those who have trusted Jesus Christ as their Saviour since Pentecost. Peter wrote that we are living stones in this temple that God is building (I Pet. 2:5). Jesus Christ built the universe, and He is building a Church.

Are you a part of what He is building? Jesus Christ is the builder, but Satan is the destroyer. Jesus said one day, "The thief [Satan] cometh not, but for to steal, and to kill, and to destroy" (John 10:10). Sin is a great destroyer, and Satan tempts people into sin. Sin destroys homes, it destroys lives, it destroys bodies. Jesus Christ came to build, not to destroy. He is the carpenter. He came to do a carpenter's work: He is building, and He is repairing.

The Lord is building a home in heaven: "I go to prepare a place for you. And if I go and prepare a place for you, I will come again, and receive you unto myself" (14:2,3). The wonderful thing about knowing Jesus as your Saviour is that you know where you are going. You may not know how long it will take to get there. We don't know if Jesus will return or if we will pass away in death—go to sleep in Jesus and wake up in heaven. This the Lord has not told us. But He has assured us that He is building a home for us in heaven. And that, to me, is a great encouragement. The Carpenter who built the universe, the Carpenter who is building His Church, is building for His Church a home in heaven.

But He is also building lives. Right now your life is either being built up by the Lord Jesus or being torn down by the Devil. There just is no middle ground. We never stand still in life. We are either growing and being built up, or we are going backward and being torn down. I think the greatest destroyer in all the universe is sin. Sin has a way of destroying people's minds, emotions and wills. Sin has a way of destroying the human body. But Jesus Christ came to build lives.

In Mark 6:2 we read that the people said, "Even such mighty works are wrought by his hands." But verse 5 says, "He could there do no mighty work, save that he laid his hands upon a few sick folk, and healed them." Why could He not work? Verse 6 tells us: "He marvelled because of their unbelief." The Lord Jesus Christ wants to build your life, and He will, if you will trust Him.

A Carpenter's Methods

There is a third reason why the Lord Jesus was a carpenter. He not only was born in a carpenter's home and came to do a carpenter's work, but He also followed a carpenter's methods. A carpenter looks at a piece of wood and sees the potential in that wood. I might not see it, but the carpenter can see it. I wonder how many times our Lord Jesus went out and cut down a tree and said, "I can see real potential in that tree."

God looks at you and says, "I see potential in you." You may look at yourself in the mirror and say, "I can never become anything, I can never do anything." Yes, you can! Jesus looked at Simon one day and said, "I know who you are. You are Simon, but I'm going to call you Peter, a rock" (see John 1:42). Peter's friends must have laughed at this, because there was not much in Peter that was like a rock. But Jesus saw the potential in Peter.

He saw the potential in Saul of Tarsus. He saw the potential in John Mark. He sees the potential in you. The Lord follows a carpenter's methods: He sees the potential that is in the material. He has a plan, and He sees the goal. God knows what He wants you to do. God knows what He wants you to become. You don't have to drift through life, wondering what to do next. Just turn yourself over to the Carpenter, and let Him fulfill His plan for you.

He is so patient! He takes such great pains in what He does. He knows just what tools to use. He knows when I have to be planed, He knows when I have to be sandpapered, and He knows when I have to be polished. He knows exactly when to use the Word of God and when to use other Christians to polish my life. The Lord Jesus follows a carpenter's methods, and He always finishes what He starts. He never leaves a job half done. But our responsibility is to surrender to Him.

A Carpenter's Death

Jesus was a carpenter because He was born into a carpenter's home. He came to do a carpenter's work—building and repairing. He followed a carpenter's methods. And finally, He died a carpenter's death. He wasn't stoned to death; He was nailed to a tree. I wonder how many times our Lord Jesus had carried trees back to the carpenter's shop and trimmed them, cured the wood, planed it and made from it some useful implement.

One day they took the Lord Jesus, and with hammers and nails—the kind of tools that He had used in the carpenter's shop—they nailed Him to a tree. Peter wrote: "Who his own self bare our sins in his own body on the tree" (I Pet. 2:24). Of course, it was not the nails that held Him to that cross; it was His love. He died a carpenter's death—nailed to a tree. Do you know why He died that death? He died that death that you and I might be saved.

Whenever you think of Jesus Christ the Carpenter, just remember the price that He paid to make something out of our lives. He had to save us from sin. Just as a carpenter has to cleanse that piece of wood—he has to cut away all that's excess, all that's ugly—so Jesus Christ, in dying for us, cleansed us from our sins. When we trust Him, He saves us. And then He begins to work in our lives to make us what we ought to be. It's a wonderful thing to know that Jesus Christ died for us.

Who is making your life? Is Satan ruining your life? You may say, "I'm a self-made man!" My friend, nobody can be a self-made man or a self-made woman. Of ourselves and in ourselves we just cannot make it. But when you put your life into the hands of the Lord Jesus, the wonderful Carpenter, He will save you, and He will make something out of you.

Yes, He is the Carpenter. He was born into a carpenter's home, so He identifies with us. He came to do a carpenter's work—to build our lives into things of beauty. He follows a carpenter's methods, patiently fulfilling the plan that He has for us. And in order to make all of this possible, He died a carpenter's death. He died for you that you might live through Him.

Perhaps just now, you would like to bow before Him and say, "Lord Jesus, You are my Saviour. Right now I trust You, I accept You. Take my life and make out of my life that which is well-pleasing in Your sight. Be my Saviour, and do it for Your glory."

Chapter 4

Our Surety

One of the titles of our Lord Jesus is used only once in the Scriptures. It is found in Hebrews 7:22: "By so much was Jesus made a surety of a better testament."

That verse is right in the middle of a rather complex chapter about the priesthood of Jesus Christ. Today the Lord Jesus Christ is our High Priest in heaven. The Old Testament priests died and so were not able to continue in their ministry. Aaron died, and his son had to take over; Eli died, and Samuel took over. But this is not so with the Lord Jesus Christ. The Lord Jesus Christ lives forever. Because He is eternal God, He will live forever. Hebrews 7:24 states, "But this man [Jesus], because he continueth ever, hath an unchangeable priesthood." So this is why He is called the believer's "surety"—He will live forever to represent us to God.

The word "surety" simply means somebody who assumes a responsibility. You have been in cities where there is a courthouse and a jail. Nearby you will always find the bondsmen—people who sell the bail bonds. They become surety for a prisoner. The judge says, "Well, you'll have to post a $1000 bond," and so the bondsman will post $1000 for the prisoner. He becomes the surety. The Greek word means "to make a pledge, to offer security." It means "to undertake an obligation for another."

One who is a surety is different from a mediator. Jesus Christ is our Mediator. A mediator gets two estranged parties together. But a mediator does not always have to pay a price. The surety is the one who is the guarantee that the price will be paid—he is the security. Our Lord Jesus Christ today is our surety in heaven.

Definition of Surety

Let's examine three different aspects of this truth. First of all, what does it mean? Why do I need a surety in heaven? I am sure you have noticed how many times in the Book of Proverbs the writer warned the reader about becoming surety. For example, in Proverbs 6 we read: "My son, if thou be surety for thy friend, if thou hast stricken thy hand with a stranger [shook hands on a deal], Thou art snared with the words of thy mouth, thou art taken with the words of thy mouth" (v. 1). He urged the man to go and deliver himself. He warned him not to become surety for a stranger because he would end up paying the bill.

I owed God a great deal; I was in debt to Him. I had broken His law, I had defied His will, and I was bankrupt—I was too poor to pay. The Lord Jesus Christ came to this earth for me, and He became poor. Second Corinthians 8:9 says, "For ye know the grace of our Lord Jesus Christ, that, though he was rich, yet for your sakes he became poor, that ye through his poverty might be rich." The Lord Jesus became poor in His birth and in His life and especially in His death. He became the poorest of the poor that He might make us the richest of the rich.

He arose from the dead and has gone back to heaven. He is alive today, and He is going to live forever because He is eternal God. There in heaven, as my High Priest, He is the surety. Do you know what that means? He is the guarantee that I am saved and that I cannot be lost.

Hebrews 7:25 tells us, "Wherefore he is able also to save them to the uttermost [forever, completely] that come unto God by him, seeing he ever liveth to make intercession for them." We often read Hebrews 7:25 as though it says He saves us *from* the uttermost. We tell people, "No matter how wicked you may be, Jesus can save you." That is true— Christ can save any sinner. But that is not what that verse is saying. The verse is not saying that Christ saves us *from* the uttermost; it is saying He saves us *to* the uttermost. He saves us *completely*. He saves us *forever*. Why? Because He is the surety.

My salvation is not wrapped up in my good works. My salvation is wrapped up in my Saviour. As long as Jesus Christ is alive, I am saved. How long is He going to live? He will live forever because He has an unchangeable priesthood. We are saved to the uttermost because Jesus is our surety.

Sometimes Satan comes to God the Father and says, "Did you see what that Christian did? Did you hear what he just said?" God the Father says, "Yes,

I did." Then God the Son says, "I am his surety. He cannot be lost because I am the guarantee that he will be saved forever." That's the explanation of this wonderful title, Jesus Christ, our surety.

Illustrations of Surety

For every New Testament doctrine, there is usually an Old Testament illustration, and this is true of the word "surety."

Joseph's Brothers

Joseph's brothers hated him and sold him into slavery (see Gen. 37—46). Joseph ended up in Egypt, but God blessed Joseph, and he became second in command in the land. A famine came, and Joseph's brothers had to go down to Egypt to get some food. Joseph recognized them, although they did not recognize him.

What did Joseph do? He wanted to make sure they would come back, so he did two things: He kept Simeon as a hostage, and he said, "If you come back, you will have to bring your youngest brother, Benjamin" (42:20). They went back and told old Jacob, and Jacob did not like it one bit. He said, "You are not going to take Benjamin! I have lost Simeon, and I have lost Joseph, and I am not going to lose Benjamin" (vv. 36-38). Then Reuben stepped up and made an offer: "Slay my two sons, if I bring him not to thee: deliver him into my hand, and I will bring him to thee again" (v. 37). But Jacob said,

"No, Reuben, I don't trust you. If you leave home, you might not come back. I might never see you again" (see v. 38).

That was all well and good until they started getting hungry again. Finally the boys said to their father, "We *have* to go back to Egypt and get some food." And then Judah stepped up and said something wonderful: "Send the lad with me, and we will arise and go; that we may live, and not die, both we, and thou, and also our little ones. I will be surety for him; of my hand shalt thou require him: if I bring him not unto thee, and set him before thee, then let me bear the blame for ever." (43:8,9). Judah said, "I will be surety for Benjamin, and I will bring him back again." And he did!

That is what the Lord Jesus Christ has done for us. He says to God the Father, "I am surety for these for whom I have died." And God the Father says, "I trust You; of course, You are a priest forever after the order of Melchizedek, and I will accept You as their surety."

Paul and Onesimus

There is also a New Testament picture of this beautiful truth. You remember that Paul wrote a little letter to a man named Philemon. Apparently Paul had led Philemon to Christ. Philemon lived, as far as we can tell, in Colossae. Philemon had a slave whose name was Onesimus. Onesimus robbed his master, fled to Rome and, by the providence of God, came in contact with Paul and was converted.

33

Paul was going to send Onesimus back to Philemon, and he wrote this in his little letter: "If thou count me therefore a partner, receive him as myself. If he hath wronged thee, or oweth thee ought [anything], put that on mine account. I Paul have written it with mine own hand, I will repay it" (Philem. 1:17-19). Paul said, "I will be surety for Onesimus. I will stand for him. When you look at Onesimus, remember that you are looking at Paul. I will pay his debt."

I like that picture. The Lord Jesus Christ is our surety in heaven. He says to God the Father, "If they owe You anything, I have paid it. Receive them the way You would receive Me."

Application of Truth

Now let's look at this truth by way of application. What does it mean to you today that Jesus Christ is your surety in heaven? Perhaps He is *not* your surety, perhaps you have never been converted, perhaps you have never trusted Christ as your Saviour. You ought to do that. And then when you trust Him as your Saviour, Jesus Christ becomes your surety in heaven. What does this mean?

God's Assurance

First, it means this: He is God's assurance that God will keep His covenant. God has made a covenant of grace with us through the Lord Jesus Christ. "By so much was Jesus made a surety of a

34

better testament" (Heb. 7:22), a better covenant. The people to whom the Book of Hebrews was written were tempted to trust in their temple, their ceremonies, their priests, their sacrifices. The writer said, "No, Jesus Christ is all that you need. He is everything. He is your hope, He is your Saviour, He is your Lord, and He is your surety." The high priest in the Jewish commonwealth died. He could not be the surety of anything. But Jesus Christ lives forever; therefore, He is God's assurance to us that God will keep His covenant.

We know that God keeps His covenant. God cannot lie, God is perfect; He will not do anything that is wrong. But just to give us that extra assurance, He says to us, "My Son is the surety. As long as He is alive, that covenant is going to be kept."

Our Assurance

Second, Christ is our assurance to God. We make promises to God, but we don't always keep them. Jesus Christ is our assurance to God. We cannot keep ourselves saved. We cannot keep ourselves perfect. Only Jesus Christ can represent us at the throne of God. He says to God the Father, "I am their surety. Whatever they owe You, I have paid. Receive them as You would receive Me, because they are My children." We as Christians have a wonderful assurance—we are not going to lose our salvation because we have a High Priest in heaven who lives forever. He stands before the

35

throne of God as the guarantee—the pledge, the security—for our salvation. He is our surety.

This truth is not given to us to make us careless. God does not give us assurance to make us careless. Anyone who is truly born again wants to live a godly life. That is why Jesus is interceding in heaven. We can come to Him at any time and know we are accepted. We can come to Him with any need and know that He will hear us. Just as Judah said, "I will be surety for that lad. I will not come home without him," so Jesus Christ says of us, "I am your surety, and you're going to get home with Me. I'm building a home for you, and you are going to make it because I am your surety."

"Wherefore he is able also to save them to the uttermost that come unto God by him, seeing he ever liveth to make intercession for them" (Heb. 7:25).

Chapter 5

Alpha and Omega

We have learned that every name Jesus wears is a blessing that He shares. The better you know Him, the more He is able to bless you. The best way to get to know Him is by studying these names and titles to find out who Jesus is and what He has done for you.

Our Lord said, "Behold, I come quickly; and my reward is with me, to give every man according as his work shall be. I am Alpha and Omega, the beginning and the end, the first and the last" (Rev. 22:12,13).

The name "Alpha and Omega" comes from the Greek alphabet. In fact, our word "alphabet" comes from the first two letters of the Greek alphabet, *alpha* and *beta*. *Alpha* is the first letter in the Greek alphabet, *omega* is the last letter. And so the Lord Jesus Christ applied the entire alphabet to Himself and said, "I am Alpha and Omega" (v. 13). This name is repeated four times in the Book of the Revelation. What truths do we learn about the Lord Jesus Christ from this name, "Alpha and Omega"?

Christ's Eternality

I think the first truth is this—His eternality. Jesus Christ is the beginning, and Jesus Christ is the

37

ending. He is the first, He is the last. This reference to Alpha and Omega in Revelation 22:13 specifically applies the name to Jesus Christ. If I stood before you and said, "I am Alpha and Omega," you would shake your head and say, "That man is just not thinking straight." But when Jesus Christ says, "I am Alpha and Omega, I am the first and the last, the beginning and the end," He is declaring Himself to be the eternal God.

In Isaiah 41:4 we read that Jehovah God said, "I the Lord, the first, and with the last; I am he." This same concept is repeated in Isaiah 44:6 and Isaiah 48:12. In other words, the Jehovah of the Old Testament is the Jesus of the New Testament. Because "Alpha and Omega" is applied to God, this means that Jesus Christ is eternal God! Our Lord Himself said in John 8:58, "Before Abraham was, I am." In Colossians 1:17 we are told, "He is before all things."

As you page through the Book of Hebrews, you will find one word repeated several times—"forever." Hebrews was written to people who wanted to hold on to their temple, their city, their priesthood and their sacrifices; but these things were not going to last forever. In fact, a few years after the book was written, the city and the temple were completely destroyed. There would be no more altar, there would be no more priesthood, there would be no more sacrifices. So why hold on to the things that are not going to last when you can build your life on the things that are really going to last?

In Hebrews 1:8 we discover that Christ's throne

is forever. No monarch on earth ever had an eternal throne, but Jesus Christ has a throne forever. We read in Hebrews 5:6: "Thou art a priest for ever." The Old Testament priests died; they had to be replaced. But not so with the Lord Jesus. Hebrews 10:14 states, "He hath perfected for ever them that are sanctified." In other words, we have a perfect salvation through faith in Jesus Christ. Hebrews 13:8 says, "Jesus Christ, the same yesterday, to day, and for ever." You and I are not the same forever; we change every day. But Jesus Christ cannot change, because He is eternal God. He cannot change for the better, because He is perfect; He certainly cannot change for the worse, because He is holy. He is the same forever. No wonder the Book of Hebrews ends with the words, "To whom be glory for ever" (13:21). "Alpha and Omega" speaks of His eternality—Jesus Christ is eternal God.

If you don't trust Jesus Christ as your Saviour, then you have no eternal salvation. Our Lord said, "If ye believe not that I am he, ye shall die in your sins" (John 8:24). Have you tied your life to that which is eternal? Or are you building your life on the changing, shifting things in this world? Nothing in this world is going to last. Only God is eternal. When you trust Jesus Christ, you receive eternal salvation—He is the author of eternal salvation to those who trust Him.

Christ's Ministry

A second truth comes from this wonderful name, and that is His ministry. What do you do with let-

39

ters? With letters you build words. Jesus Christ is the Word. "In the beginning was the Word, and the Word was with God, and the Word was God. The same was in the beginning with God" (John 1:1,2). "And the Word was made flesh, . . . and we beheld his glory" (v. 14). The Lord Jesus Christ is God's eternal Word.

Once again I go back to the Book of Hebrews. One of its major themes is this: "God has spoken, and what are you going to do about it?" The book begins, "God, who at sundry times and in divers manners spake in times past . . . hath in these last days spoken unto us by his Son" (1:1,2). Toward the end, the Book of Hebrews says, "See that ye refuse not him that speaketh" (12:25). What will you do with the Word of God?

Jesus Christ is Alpha and Omega—He is the alphabet of God's revelation. And from the alphabet of God's revelation He builds the Word. If you want to understand God, you have to know Jesus Christ. I have met people who say, "Well, I get so much truth about God from walking in the woods." You can learn some things about God by walking in the woods, but you cannot get the full revelation you have in Christ. Some say, "I love to sit and look at a beautiful sunset; it tells me so much about God." Well, it can; but you will learn much more of God's revelation through His Son, Jesus Christ. God has spoken in Jesus Christ, and this is His last word. Jesus Christ is God's last word, and if you want to know about God, you have to come to Jesus Christ. Jesus Christ is Alpha and Omega; His ministry is the ministry of revelation—He reveals God to us.

In the upper room one of the apostles said to Jesus, in effect, "Lord, show us the Father, and we'll be satisfied" (see John 14:8). Jesus replied, "Have I been so long time with you, and yet hast thou not known me, Philip? he that hath seen me hath seen the Father" (v. 9). This is Alpha and Omega, this is His ministry of revelation. He is God's alphabet of grace, revealing the heart and the mind of God that we might know Him and become like Him.

Christ's Sufficiency

There is a third truth that is found in this name "Alpha and Omega"—not only His eternality and His ministry but also His sufficiency. In the English language we say, "He has everything from A to Z." Well, the Greeks would say, "He has everything from *alpha* to *omega*—He is all-sufficient." When Jesus says He is Alpha and Omega, He is saying, "I am sufficient; there is nothing missing, I am all that you need."

In recent weeks I have been studying Paul's letter to the Colossians, and I have noticed that 32 times in this little letter Paul used the word "all." We read in Colossians 1:16: "For by him were all things created." Verse 17 says, "He is before all things, and by him all things consist [hold together]." We read in verse 18: "That in all things he might have the preeminence." And verse 19 says, "For it pleased the Father that in him should all fulness dwell."

41

Colossians 2:3 states, "In whom are hid all the treasures of wisdom and knowledge." Colossians 2:9 says, "For in him dwelleth all the fulness of the Godhead bodily." You ask, "What does that mean to me?" Colossians 2:10 tells us what it means to us: "And ye are complete in him." You are made full in Him.

Did you know that when you trusted Christ as your Saviour, you were introduced to eternal sufficiency? Everything you ever need you can get from Jesus Christ. You are rich in Him. He comes to you and says, "What is it you need? Just spell it out to Me. I am Alpha and Omega; I am adequate for every situation; I am sufficient for every need." That is what the grace of God is all about. The grace of God means that God is adequate for every need.

You may be hurting today. You may be facing a rather dismal situation, because of bad news or bad circumstances. You may feel very inadequate. If you know Jesus Christ as your Saviour, you have His sufficiency. Whatever your need is today, He is adequate to meet it.

Christ's Victory

There is a fourth lesson I want to share with you, and it's this: "Alpha and Omega" not only means His eternality, His ministry and His sufficiency, but it also means His victory. Whatever He starts, He finishes. I confess to you I have in my files work that I have started and have never finished. I have books that I have begun to write but have never completed. Jesus Christ finishes everything He starts. The Book of the Revelation reveals that to us. In Genesis we read of the creation of the heavens and the earth; Revelation speaks of the new heavens and the new earth. The Book of Genesis speaks of Satan's attack on God's creation, when man fell into sin; the Book of the Revelation tells how Satan will be bound and then judged forever. The Book of the Revelation is the completion of the Book of Genesis. What God starts He finishes. What God starts in our lives He will finish.

Sometimes it looks as though God is not going to make it, but He is going to make it, and His will shall be accomplished. Be encouraged today! Christ is Alpha and Omega, and if you begin with Him at Alpha, you will end with Him at Omega! He is the beginning and the end, He is the first and the last. "Looking unto Jesus the author and finisher of our faith" (Heb. 12:2). Philippians 1:6 reminds us that "he which hath begun a good work in you will perform [complete] it until the day of Jesus Christ."

"Alpha and Omega" means His eternality, His ministry, His sufficiency and His victory. Let's be encouraged today, for He is Alpha and Omega, and He is our Saviour.

Chapter 6

The Lamb

One of the great names of the Lord Jesus Christ in the Bible is the "Lamb." From the beginning to the end of the Word of God, we find Jesus Christ the Lamb.

A key verse concerning the Lamb of God is John 1:29: "The next day John seeth Jesus coming unto him, and saith, Behold the Lamb of God, which taketh away the sin of the world." We are going to consider four phrases from the Bible that summarize what the Word of God has to say about Jesus Christ the Lamb.

"Where Is the Lamb?"

The first phrase is a question found in Genesis 22:7, where Isaac asked, "Where is the lamb?" God had said to Abraham, "Take now thy son, thine only son Isaac, whom thou lovest, and get thee into the land of Moriah; and offer him there for a burnt-offering upon one of the mountains which I will tell thee of" (v. 2). Every statement in that verse tugs at our hearts. "Take now thy son, thine only son Isaac [laughter], whom thou lovest." Abraham took his son, Isaac, who was probably a young man at this time, to sacrifice him on an altar.

44

Of course, our loving Father in heaven never asks for human sacrifices. Throughout the Old Testament He condemned the Jewish people when they imitated their pagan neighbors by giving their children as sacrifices. God did not want Isaac's life—He wanted Abraham's heart. Isaac logically asked the question, "Where is the lamb?" (v. 7).

This question was asked throughout the Old Testament period: "Where is the Lamb?" Abraham's answer was a good one: "My son, God will provide himself a lamb for a burnt-offering" (v. 8). And when Abraham placed Isaac on the altar and was about to kill him, God provided a ram that took Isaac's place. But Abraham was looking far beyond Mount Moriah; he was looking to Mount Calvary. That is why he answered, "God will provide himself a lamb," not only for a burnt offering but also for a sin offering, a peace offering and a trespass offering. Jesus Christ came and fulfilled all of those Old Testament sacrifices.

Years later, the Israelites went into Egypt, suffered in slavery and then were delivered by Moses. At the Exodus, the lamb again played an important role. In Exodus 12:3 Moses said, "They shall take to them every man a lamb, according to the house." Verse 4 says, "If the household be too little for the lamb." Verse 5 says, "Your lamb." That is an interesting progression: *a* lamb, *the* lamb, *your* lamb.

"Behold the Lamb"

Isaiah 53:7 gives us a wonderful answer to that question, "Where is the Lamb?" The prophet said,

45

"He was oppressed, and he was afflicted, yet he opened not his mouth: he is brought as a lamb to the slaughter, and as a sheep before her shearers is dumb, so he openeth not his mouth." Where is the Lamb? That was the great question in the Old Testament period.

The question was answered by John the Baptist in John 1:29. John the Baptist pointed to Jesus and said, "Behold the Lamb of God, which taketh away the sin of the world." That was a very important statement, and every phrase in that statement tells us something about the Lord Jesus.

The Lamb

John said, "Behold *the* Lamb" (John 1:29). In the Old Testament period, there had been *many* lambs—thousands of lambs were slain every Passover. In fact, at the tabernacle and in the temple, at least two lambs were killed every day. Add to these the special sacrifices that were brought by the people, and you can well imagine that millions of lambs had been slain by John the Baptist's time. But he said, "Behold *the* Lamb." This was the final Lamb—once and for all a sacrifice was going to be made that would solve the sin problem.

God's Lamb

Furthermore, this is the Lamb of *God:* "Behold the Lamb of God" (John 1:29). This is not man's lamb. Man did not want Him. He was rejected by

His own people. His own relatives did not understand Him. "He came unto his own, and his own received him not" (v. 11). He was not man's choice, He was *God's* choice. "He is despised and rejected of men; a man of sorrows, and acquainted with grief" (Isa. 53:3).

Because He was God's Lamb, He was perfect. At the Passover time, the Israelites had to pen up their lambs and watch them to make sure they were perfect. They could not bring to the Lord a sacrifice that was not perfect. The Lord Jesus Christ was examined from every side. The demons admitted He was the Son of God. Pilate said, "I find no fault in this man" (Luke 23:4). Even Judas said he had betrayed "innocent blood" (Matt. 27:4). The soldier said, "Truly this was the Son of God" (v. 54). The Lord Jesus Christ was examined on every side, and they discovered He was "holy, harmless, undefiled" (Heb. 7:26). He was "a lamb without blemish and without spot" (I Pet. 1:19). Spots come from defilement on the outside; blemishes come from decay on the inside. On the outside and on the inside, Jesus Christ, God's Lamb, was perfect.

Takes Away Sin

Jesus the Lamb *takes away sin*. There was not a lamb in the entire Old Testament period that took away sin. The blood of a sacrifice could *cover* sin, but the blood of a sacrifice never *took away* sin. "For it is not possible that the blood of bulls and of goats should take away sins" (Heb. 10:4). Those

47

sacrifices were animal sacrifices, and the blood of an animal cannot deal with the sin of a human being who is made in the image of God. Furthermore, those animals were not willing; those were not voluntary sacrifices. No lamb ever volunteered to die. But when Jesus Christ came, He was voluntarily the sacrifice for our sin, and His blood takes away sin. There is complete and final forgiveness. "Their sins and their iniquities will I remember no more" (8:12).

One Lamb—not many lambs; *God's* Lamb—not man's lamb; a Lamb whose blood *takes away sin*—not a lamb whose blood simply covers sin.

The World's Sin

Notice in John 1:29 that the Lamb of God takes away the sin of *the world.* A ram died for Isaac (see Gen. 22). That was a sacrifice for the *individual.* In Exodus 12, the Israelites selected a lamb for each *household.* In Isaiah 53:7,8 we are told that the Lord Jesus Christ is God's Lamb who died for the sins of His *nation:* "For the transgression of my people was he stricken." So there was a lamb for the individual, a lamb for the household and a Lamb for the nation. But Jesus Christ was also a Lamb *for the whole world*—He takes away the sin of the world.

That is why we have a missionary outreach. You and I are, or should be, concerned about getting out the gospel because we have a Saviour whose sacrifice can take care of the sins of the world.

48

"Worthy Is the Lamb"

A third statement concerning the Lamb is found in Revelation 5:12: "Worthy is the Lamb." Revelation 5 records the worship of heaven. All of the choirs of heaven sing. "Ten thousand times ten thousand, and thousands of thousands" (v. 11) say with a loud voice, "Worthy is the Lamb" (v. 12). This Lamb, of course, is Jesus Christ.

More than 25 times in the Book of the Revelation He is called the "Lamb." And John did not use the ordinary word for "lamb," he used the word meaning "a little pet lamb." "Worthy is the Lamb that was slain to receive power, and riches, and wisdom, and strength, and honour, and glory, and blessing" (v. 12).

"Where is the Lamb? That is the question of the ages. "Behold the Lamb" (John 1:29) is the answer to the question. "Worthy is the Lamb" (Rev. 5:12) is our worshipful response. What a delight it is just to worship the Lord Jesus and to praise Him because He died for us.

"Hide Us From . . . the Lamb"

There is a fourth statement about the Lamb, found in Revelation 6:15,16. The Lamb will open the seals in heaven, and judgment will come. "And the kings of the earth, and the great men, and the rich men, and the chief captains, and the mighty men, and every bondman, and every free man, hid themselves in the dens and in the rocks of the mountains; and said to the mountains and rocks, Fall on us, and hide us from the face of him that sitteth on the throne, and from the wrath of the Lamb." What a statement! "Hide us . . . from the wrath of the Lamb" (v. 16).

No one ever thinks of a lamb as being full of wrath. We think of a lamb in terms of weakness and humility. But in Revelation 6 we are told that the day is coming when unbelievers, people who have rejected Jesus Christ, are going to cry out in fear and try to hide from the face of the Lamb. I trust that will not be true in your life. I trust you will not say, "Hide us from the face . . . of the Lamb" (v. 16). I trust that you are saying, "Worthy is the Lamb" (5:12) and that you are praising Him.

Everything in the Book of the Revelation relates to the Lamb. The throne is the throne of the Lamb. The temple is the temple of the Lamb. The light in the city is the Lamb: "The Lamb is the light thereof" (21:23). The marriage is the marriage of the Lamb. And the book that has the names of the saved people in it is the Lamb's book. Have you trusted the Lamb of God who takes away sin? Has He taken away your sin? Just ask Him by faith to save you, because He is the Lamb of God who takes away the sin of the world.

Where is the Lamb? That question need not be asked anymore because John the Baptist answered it for us: "Behold the Lamb" (John 1:29). If you have seen Him by faith, if you have trusted Him, then you are saying in your heart and with your lips, "Worthy is the Lamb" (Rev. 5:12). But if you have not trusted

Him, one day you will say, "Hide us . . . from the wrath of the Lamb: For the great day of his wrath is come" (6:16).

Chapter 7

The Firstborn

"And so it was, that, while they were there, the days were accomplished that she should be delivered. And she brought forth her firstborn son, and wrapped him in swaddling clothes, and laid him in a manger; because there was no room for them in the inn" (Luke 2:6,7).

Several times in the New Testament the title "firstborn" is applied to the Lord Jesus. To us who are Gentiles, "firstborn" does not mean a great deal; but it meant a great deal to the Jews, because the firstborn son had many rights and privileges. However, in the New Testament "firstborn" does not necessarily mean "born first." In the case of the Lord Jesus, He was Mary's firstborn Son. He was conceived by the Holy Spirit and born of the virgin Mary. According to Mark 6:3, Mary and Joseph also had children. After our Lord Jesus was born, they lived as husband and wife. But our Lord was born in a very special way. Joseph was His foster father, not His literal father. Mary gave birth to the Lord Jesus, and He was literally her firstborn.

But the term "firstborn" in the Bible carries with it the idea of superiority and priority. Whoever was firstborn was designated as the very special one. The firstborn got the inheritance. In Exodus 4:22 we read that God designated the people of Israel as His firstborn. So if we think of the word "firstborn" as meaning "priority, superiority, the highest of the high," we will have no problem applying this title to the Lord Jesus Christ.

When you consider all of the references where the term "firstborn" applies to Jesus, you understand four different aspects of His Person and His work. "Who is the image of the invisible God, the firstborn of every creature" (Col. 1:15). "And he is the head of the body, the church: who is the beginning, the firstborn from the dead; that in all things he might have the preeminence" (v. 18). "For whom he did foreknow, he also did predestinate to be conformed to the image of his Son, that he [His Son] might be the firstborn among many brethren" (Rom. 8:29). "And again, when he bringeth in the firstbegotten [firstborn] into the world, he saith, And let all the angels of God worship him" (Heb. 1:6). Let us consider these four references and learn the significance of Jesus Christ's being the firstborn.

"First-born of All Creation"

First of all, He is "the first-born of all creation" (Col. 1:15, NASB). The theme of Colossians is the preeminence of Jesus Christ: "That in all things he [Jesus Christ] might have the preeminence" (v. 18). "But Christ is all, and in all" (3:11). In Colossians 1, we see the preeminence of the Lord Jesus Christ in salvation: "Giving thanks unto the Father, which hath made us meet [fit] to be partakers of the

53

inheritance of the saints in light: . . . In whom we have redemption through his blood, even the forgiveness of sins" (vv. 12,14). Our Lord is preeminent in salvation.

He is also preeminent in creation. Verse 16 tells us, "By him were all things created." If that is the case, then He Himself was not created. Some want us to believe that Jesus Christ was a created being—the highest of the created beings, but not eternal God. But verse 16 says, "For by him were all things created." Therefore He Himself is not a created thing. "All things . . . that are in heaven, and that are in earth, visible and invisible, whether they be thrones, or dominions, or principalities, or powers: all things were created by him, and for him: and he is before all things" (vv. 16,17). That is another proof that He is not a created being. "He is before all things, and by him all things consist [hold together]" (v. 17). Jesus Christ is preeminent in creation.

What does it mean to be the firstborn of all creation? It means to be the highest of everything in creation. Remember, "firstborn" carries with it the idea of priority, superiority, the highest of the high, the one who is going to share in the inheritance. The Lord Jesus Christ is superior to everything in creation because He existed prior to creation. "All things were made by him" (John 1:3). "All things were created by him, and for him" (Col. 1:16), and all things hold together by His power. This makes Him the highest of the high in all of creation.

Why are we having problems with creation today? We have problems with pollution. We have

54

ecological problems that are leading to economic problems which, in turn, are leading to political problems. Do you know why we have these problems? Primarily, it is because we do not believe in creation anymore. We have taken Jesus Christ out of His place of preeminence as the firstborn of all creation. As a result, we have ugliness instead of beauty; we have destructiveness instead of growth and construction; there is waste, and there is idolatry. People worship the things of creation, the things that they manufacture. When Jesus Christ is given His proper place as the firstborn of all creation, these problems will be solved, and we will look upon creation as something He has made to be used to glorify Him. He is the firstborn of all creation.

We look forward to that day when Jesus is going to come again and all of creation will be delivered from bondage and corruption. We will have beauty and harmony, glory and blessing, because the firstborn of all creation, Jesus Christ, will be reigning supremely.

"Firstborn From the Dead"

Jesus Christ is not only the firstborn of all creation, but He is also the first begotten, or the firstborn, from the dead (Col. 1:18). This same title is used in Revelation 1:5. This does not mean that Jesus Christ was the first one raised from the dead; we know He was not. In the Old Testament days there were people who were raised from the dead.

We have the record of Jesus' raising at least three people from the dead, and possibly He raised more. Why, then, is He called the firstborn from the dead?

Raised Himself

He is the highest of those who have been raised from the dead. He is the greatest—He stands supremely above everyone else. Our Lord Jesus Christ knew He was going to be raised from the dead. He announced it to His disciples. Not only that, He raised Himself from the dead. He said, "I have power [authority] to lay it down, I have power [authority] to take it again" (John 10:18). Lazarus did not raise himself from the dead (John 11:1-44). That little daughter of Jairus did not raise herself from the dead (Mark 5:21-43). The son of that widow at Nain did not raise himself from the dead (Luke 7:11-18). But Jesus raised Himself from the dead. He is the highest of all who have ever been raised from the dead.

Never to Die Again

Second, He was raised from the dead by His own power, never to die again. Lazarus died again, Jairus's daughter died again, and the son of the widow of Nain died again. But the Lord Jesus lives and never will die. He had the power to lay down His life; He had the power to take it up again, and now He lives an endless life. Being raised from the dead, He is now reigning in heaven, and death cannot reach

Him. He is the firstborn from among the dead, the highest and the greatest, because He raised Himself, never to die again.

Can and Will Raise Others

And He raised Himself that He might be able to raise others. Lazarus never raised anybody. We have no record in Scripture that anyone who was raised from the dead ever raised anybody else. But Jesus did. And Jesus will again. Christ is the One in glory who possesses endless life and who "brought life and immortality to light through the gospel" (II Tim. 1:10). You and I never need to fear death because we are trusting Him who is the firstborn from the dead. He has conquered death. Death could not hold Him, and death will not hold us when He calls us to come to be with Him.

"Firstborn Among Many Brethren"

Romans 8:29 is the third reference to Jesus Christ as the firstborn: "For whom he did foreknow, he also did predestinate to be conformed to the image of his Son, that he might be the firstborn among many brethren."

Our Lord Jesus Christ does not want to keep all these blessings to Himself. Someone has said that God loves His Son so much that He wants everybody else to be just like Him. One day you and I are going to experience this. We shall see Him, and "we shall be like him; for we shall see him as he is"

(I John 3:2). If you know Jesus as your Saviour, you are one of His "many brethren." One day you will be like Him, for He is "the firstborn among many brethren" (Rom. 8:29). What He is we one day shall be.

The Church is called "the church of the firstborn" (Heb. 12:23). In one sense, we are the Church of the "second-born." In my first birth, God would not accept me; but I have had a second birth whereby I received eternal life, and one day I shall be like Jesus Christ. If you belong to Jesus Christ, you belong to the Church of the firstborn, the highest, the most privileged. One day you will share in His glory. He is "the firstborn among many brethren," and one day we are going to be like Him.

When is this going to happen? Hebrews 1:6 gives the answer. The writer was referring to our Lord's coming. "And again, when he bringeth in the first-begotten into the world, he saith, And let all the angels of God worship him." Some Bible students disagree on this verse, but I believe that that word "again" refers to when Jesus comes again. When He brings the firstbegotten into the world, He says, "And let all the angels of God worship him." I think this applies to when our Lord Jesus shall return for His Church. When He came the first time to this earth, the angels did worship Him; but He came in humility. When He comes again, He is going to come in glory. When He came the first time and was born in Bethlehem, He came in weakness as a little baby; but He is going to come again in power and great glory. He came to provide salvation when He came to Bethlehem; but when He comes again, there will be judgment. When He came the first time, He ended up with a crown of thorns; but when He comes again, He will wear a crown of victory.

Jesus Christ is God's firstborn. He is going to inherit all things. He is to have all the glory and honor. I trust that you know Him as your Saviour so that you will share in this eternal inheritance.

Chapter 8

Emmanuel

Let's consider a title of our Lord Jesus Christ that is used only once in the New Testament and twice in the Old Testament. You will find the New Testament reference in Matthew 1:23, a quotation from Isaiah 7:14: "Behold, a virgin shall be with child, and shall bring forth a son, and they shall call his name Emmanuel, which being interpreted is, God with us."

The background for this prediction takes us back 700 years before the birth of the Lord Jesus (see Isa. 7—9). Ahaz was the king of Judah. He was not a very godly man, and he was threatened by Syria and Israel. Those two nations were going to attack him. Isaiah the prophet encouraged King Ahaz to trust in the Lord, and Ahaz outwardly said he would trust in the Lord. But secretly, Ahaz allied himself with Assyria, the enemy of his nation. In other words, he was a hypocrite. Outwardly he said, "Yes, I will trust the Lord," but behind everybody's back, he was lining up some military support from Assyria. Isaiah encouraged him by telling him, "Immanuel [God with us]" (7:14). God offered to give Ahaz a sign, but the king refused. So God gave a sign, not just to Ahaz the king but to all the people of Israel and Judah. The sign was that the virgin would conceive and would bring forth a Son, and this Son would be "God with us." This prophecy was fulfilled in the birth of our Lord Jesus Christ.

Joseph, a just man, was about to divorce the girl to whom he was engaged. In the Jewish culture, engagement involved a very strong commitment—it was the next thing to marriage. If you were going to break an engagement, it was technically a divorce. Joseph had discovered that Mary was with child, so he had decided to break their engagement. Then the angel spoke to Joseph, and told him that Mary was faithful but was carrying a child which had been conceived by the Holy Spirit. She would "bring forth a son, and they shall call his name Emmanuel." "Emmanuel" means "God with us."

Jesus never used this name. We don't find anyone in the four Gospels ever calling Him by this name. It is really a title, a description of who He is. There are two very wonderful truths that are wrapped up in this title.

Jesus Is God

First of all, Jesus is God. "They shall call his name Emmanuel, which being interpreted is, God with us" (Matt. 1:23). There are those who tell us that Jesus is not God, that He was simply a godly man or a very godly teacher. Yet from the very beginning of the New Testament, Jesus Christ is identified as God. If I called myself Emmanuel and told you that I was God, you would think I was crazy—and rightly

61

so! But the New Testament writers applied to Jesus Christ the title "Emmanuel, . . . God with us."

Claimed to Be God

Jesus Christ claimed to be God, and He did so at the risk of His own life. In John 10:30 we read the words that Jesus said: "I and my Father are one." That statement is the next thing to saying, "I am God." "Then the Jews took up stones again to stone him. Jesus answered them, Many good works have I shewed you from my Father; for which of those works do ye stone me? The Jews answered him, saying, For a good work we stone thee not; but for blasphemy; and because that thou, being a man, makest thyself God" (vv. 31-33). They understood by His statement "I and my Father are one" that He was claiming to be God.

In John 14 we read that the Lord Jesus Christ was asked by Philip: "Shew us the Father, and it sufficeth us" (v. 8). Jesus said, "Have I been so long time with you, and yet hast thou not known me, Philip? he that hath seen me hath seen the Father" (v. 9). So Jesus claimed to be God. This is why they crucified Him.

The Jews told Pilate, "We have a law, and by our law he ought to die, because he made himself the Son of God" (19:7). The Jewish people had no problem understanding what He was talking about. Jesus claimed to be God.

More than that, Jesus received worship as God. If you worship any creature, that is idolatry. It is commanded: "Thou shalt worship the Lord thy God, and him only shalt thou serve" (Matt. 4:10). In Matthew 2:11 we read that the Magi came and worshiped Him. When Jesus walked on the water and calmed the great storm, the disciples bowed down and worshiped Him (see 14:22-33). In John 9:38 we learn that the blind man whom Jesus healed worshiped Him.

And Jesus accepted this worship! This means He knew He was God. So He claimed to be God, and He received worship as God.

Called God

A number of times in the New Testament, He is specifically called God. Let's note these references. John 1:1 says, "In the beginning was the Word, and the Word was with God, and the Word was God." "Word" refers to Jesus Christ because verse 14 says, "And the Word was made flesh, and dwelt among us."

In John 1:18, our Lord Jesus Christ is called God. The King James Version says, "No man hath seen God at any time; the only begotten Son, which is in the bosom of the Father, he hath declared [unfolded, shown forth] him." The only way He could do that is to be God Himself. The New International Version translates this verse, "God the only Son, who is at the Father's side." The New American Standard Bible translates it, "The only begotten God, who is in the bosom of the Father."

In Romans 9:5, where the Apostle Paul was describing the nation of Israel, we read: "Whose are the fathers, and of whom as concerning the flesh Christ came, who is over all, God blessed for ever." Titus 2:13 is very clear: "Looking for that blessed hope, and the glorious appearing of the great God and our Saviour Jesus Christ." There is only one article in the Greek—"the great God and our Saviour." Our Saviour is God! In Hebrews 1:8 we read that God the Father says to God the Son, "Thy throne, O God, is for ever and ever." Second Peter 1:1 reads: "Simon Peter, a servant and an apostle of Jesus Christ, to them that hath obtained like precious faith with us through the righteousness of God and our Saviour Jesus Christ." One Person, two titles: "God and our Saviour Jesus Christ."

First John 5:20 to me is a real clincher: "And we know that the Son of God is come and hath given us an understanding, that we may know him that is true, and we are in him that is true, even in his Son Jesus Christ. This is the true God, and eternal life." Our Lord Jesus Christ is God!

Jesus Is God With Us

There is a second truth that comes from the name "Emmanuel." Not only is He God, but He is God with us. He is not a God who is far away, distant and unconcerned; He is with us. When

Jesus Christ was born of the virgin Mary and came into this world as a little baby, He identified with humanity. He is the God-Man; He is God, and He is God with us. Often in the Bible you find that wonderful promise, "I am with you." God gave that promise to Moses, and He gave it to Joshua. He said, "As I was with Moses, so I will be with thee" (Josh. 1:5). He has given that same promise to us. Matthew began his Gospel by introducing "God with us" (1:23), and he ended his book on the same note. Matthew 28:20 says, "Lo, I am with you alway, even unto the end of the world [age]." The Lord Jesus Christ is God with us in every area of life.

In Salvation

He is with us in salvation. He is a holy God, and He ought to be against us because we are unholy people. But He is with us in salvation. If you will open your heart to Him, He will come in, and He will be with you. He will forgive you; He will fellowship with you.

In Trials

He is with us in the trials of life. How many times I have turned to Isaiah 43:2, and I have read for my own benefit this promise: "When thou passest through the waters, I will be with thee; and through the rivers, they shall not overflow thee: when thou walkest through the fire, thou shalt not be burned; neither shall the flame kindle upon thee." Verse 5 says, "Fear not: for I am with thee." In Isaiah 41:10 we read: "Fear thou not; for I am with thee: be not dismayed; for I am thy God: I will strengthen thee; yea, I will help thee; yea, I will uphold thee with the right hand of my righteousness." No matter what circumstances we go through, Jesus Christ is with us.

In Our Service

He is with us in our service, as we seek to serve Him and to do His will. "And they went forth, and preached every where, the Lord working with them" (Mark 16:20). Not only is He walking with us, but He is also working with us. There are times when we get weary in the Lord's work. We do not get weary of the Lord's work, because it is exciting, and we are thrilled with the privileges we have to serve Him. But sometimes we get weary in the Lord's work. It is good to know that the Lord is working with us.

When Paul was getting that church started in Corinth (Acts 18), he was ready to quit. Then the Lord appeared to him and said, "Now don't be afraid, Paul; I am with you" (see v. 9). The Lord stood with Paul to the very end of his ministry, even though some of his friends forsook him.

In Sorrows and in Eternity

Christ is with us in the sorrows of life, as we go through bereavement and tears and separation.

66

The promise is in Psalm 23:4: "Yea, though I walk through the valley of the shadow of death, I will fear no evil, for thou art with me." He is with us in the sorrows of life, and He is going to be with us throughout all eternity. In Revelation 21, John saw that Holy City coming down from heaven, and he heard a great voice saying, "Behold, the tabernacle of God is with men, and he will dwell with them, and they shall be his people, and God himself shall be with them, and be their God" (v. 3). "Emmanuel, . . . God with us" (Matt. 1:23).

Jesus Christ is God; trust Him, worship Him, give your very best to Him. And *Jesus Christ is God with us.* Wherever we are, in the difficulties and demands of life, Jesus Christ is right there. "Emmanuel, . . . God with us." Are you trusting Him today? Have you surrendered your all to Him? This is what He wants us to do, for He is God with us.

Chapter 9

Jesus

"And the angel said unto her, Fear not, Mary: for thou hast found favour with God. And, behold, thou shalt conceive in thy womb, and bring forth a son, and shalt call his name Jesus" (Luke 1:30,31). We come now to that name which means the most to all of us who are saved, the name "Jesus."

A sociologist once made a study of names. He studied the names of 15,000 juvenile delinquents, and he discovered an interesting thing: Those young people who had strange or embarrassing names had four times as much trouble as all the others. This man concluded that there were about 5000 safe names that you could give to a child.

The name you give to your child may not determine his or her destiny, but the name that was given to our Lord was a part of His destiny. "Thou shalt call his name Jesus: for he shall save his people from their sins" (Matt. 1:21). I suppose that, in our society, there are two names that no one would use today. One is "Judas," because that name is too terrible; the other is "Jesus," because that name is too wonderful.

Sometimes the name "Jesus" is used in blasphemy. Sometimes it's sung or spoken rather carelessly and casually. Yet "Jesus" is a very special name. Let me share four facts with you that help us to better understand the wonder of that name.

Given From Heaven

Fact number one: The name of Jesus is *a name given from heaven.* Whenever we had a child, we had to answer the question "What shall we call the baby?" I have some friends who waited five or six days before naming their last child, and the hospital was somewhat perturbed about this. With the Lord Jesus, there was no problem because the name was given from heaven.

First, the angel gave the name to the mother, Mary. We read that in Luke 1:31: "And, behold, thou shalt conceive in thy womb, and bring forth a son, and shalt call his name Jesus." Then the name was given to Joseph, the foster father of Jesus. Joseph considered putting Mary away because he thought she had sinned. But God said, "Joseph, thou son of David, fear not to take unto thee Mary thy wife: for that which is conceived in her is of the Holy Ghost. And she shall bring forth a son, and thou shalt call his name Jesus: for he shall save his people from their sins" (Matt. 1:20,21). It was a name given from heaven.

This is logical, because the Lord Jesus Christ came from heaven. Many times in the Gospel of John, Jesus talked about coming down from heaven, coming from the Father. The Lord Jesus Christ did not come into this world the way you and I came. We had an earthly father and an earthly mother.

69

Our Lord Jesus had an earthly mother but not an earthly father. The Holy Spirit conceived Jesus in the womb of Mary, because He came into the world from heaven. Every baby that is born into this world is a person who has never existed before. But when Jesus came into this world, He had existed from all eternity; so His birth had to be different. He came from heaven, and therefore His name was given from heaven.

He came to do a work that only heaven could do—salvation. "For God so loved the world, that he gave his only begotten Son, that whosoever believeth in him should not perish, but have everlasting life. For God sent not his Son into the world to condemn the world; but that the world through him might be saved" (John 3:16,17). He came to do the work that only heaven could do—save lost sinners. Salvation is of the Lord, because no man can save himself.

His name was given from heaven because one day He is going to take His people to heaven. "I go to prepare a place for you. And if I go and prepare a place for you, I will come again, and receive you unto myself; that where I am, there ye may be also" (14:2,3). The name of Jesus was a name given from heaven.

Great in History

Fact number two: The name of Jesus is *a name great in history*. The name "Jesus" is the Greek form of "Joshua," or "Jehoshua," which means "Jehovah is salvation."

Joshua the Conqueror

Two great men in the Old Testament had this name. One was Joshua, the conqueror. You will remember that Joshua was the man who assisted Moses, and then he replaced Moses. Joshua led the people into the Promised Land where they claimed their inheritance. In Numbers 13:8 we have his name given as "Oshea," or "Hoshea," which means "salvation." But Moses changed his name from "Hoshea" to "Jehoshua," which means "Jehovah is salvation" (v. 16).

Many Jewish people enjoyed giving their sons that name. When a little boy was born into a Jewish home and they wanted him to become a great conqueror, they named him "Joshua, Jehovah is salvation." Joshua is a picture of our Lord Jesus Christ, according to Hebrews 4:8. Joshua followed Moses. Moses represented the Law, but Joshua represented the victory that comes by grace. This reminds me of John 1:17: "For the law was given by Moses, but grace and truth came by Jesus Christ." Joshua conquered the enemy and led the people into their inheritance.

The Law cannot give anyone an inheritance. It is not possible through the keeping of the Law to enter into the inheritance of God, the "rest" that we have through faith in Jesus Christ. Joshua, not Moses, led the people into their rest. It is Jesus who

71

gives us rest. He is our Joshua. He has conquered all of our enemies. The last enemy, death, has been conquered by the Lord Jesus. When you know Jesus as your Saviour, you have entered into your inheritance, you are enriched in Him, you have all spiritual blessings through Him. He says, "Come unto me, . . . and I will give you rest" (Matt. 11:28). Jesus Christ is our Joshua—"Jehoshua, Jehovah is salvation."

Joshua the High Priest

The second person in the Old Testament who had this name was Joshua, the high priest. You will find him mentioned in Zechariah 3. The Lord Jesus Christ is, of course, our High Priest. He is a High Priest after the order of Melchizedek, according to Hebrews 5:10 and 6:20.

Melchizedek was that interesting man found in Genesis 14. There is no record of his ancestry. He met Abraham after Abraham had won that great battle. He is a picture of Jesus Christ, our King-Priest.

Joshua, the high priest, pictured the priesthood of the Lord Jesus Christ. Joshua, the conqueror, and Joshua, the high priest—these were two great men in Jewish history. The name "Jesus" is a name given from heaven and a name great in history.

Glorious in Honor

Fact number three: "Jesus" is *a name glorious in honor.* It is interesting that even though "Joshua," or "Jesus," was a common name among the Jews, they stopped using it after about the second century. It seems that the Lord Jesus Christ had taken that name and done something to it, as far as they were concerned. Jesus was known as "Jesus of Nazareth," to distinguish Him from all the other people who were named "Jesus" (or "Joshua") in that day. Or He was called "Jesus the Christ." He took that name and lifted it to the highest heavens: "Wherefore God also hath highly exalted him, and given him a name which is above every name: That at the name of Jesus every knee should bow, of things in heaven, and things in earth, and things under the earth; and that every tongue should confess that Jesus Christ is Lord, to the glory of God the Father" (Phil. 2:9-11). It's a name glorious in honor. Do you know why?

Jesus Christ meets our greatest need. What is your greatest need? Salvation from sin, victory over sin. He meets that need. To do this, He paid the greatest price: He died on the cross, arose again and went back to heaven. He secured for us the greatest blessings. Whatever blessings you need, you can find them in Jesus Christ—blessings that will last forever. Yes, the name of Jesus is a name given from heaven, a name great in history, a name glorious in honor.

Gracious in Help

Fact number four: It is *a name gracious in help.* Whenever people heard the name "Jesus," they knew what it meant: "Jehovah is salvation." The Lord Jesus came "to seek and to save that which was lost" (Luke 19:10). In Mark 10:46-52, blind Bartimaeus was sitting by the roadside. He heard a crowd going by, and his ears told him there was something different about that crowd. And he said, "What is happening? Who is going by?" They replied, "Jesus of Nazareth is passing by." "Salvation" was passing by! "Jehovah is salvation" was passing by. You will recall that Bartimaeus cried out and said, "Jesus, thou son of David, have mercy on me" (v. 47). And the Lord Jesus cured him and saved him.

That thief on the cross saw a sign above the head of Jesus: "This Is Jesus The King Of The Jews" (Matt. 27:37)—Jesus, Saviour! The Lord Jesus is gracious in His help. Through the name of Jesus we can have salvation. Through the name of Jesus we pray. In the name of Jesus Christ we are able to conquer the Evil One.

You may ask, "Isn't there anybody else who can do this?" No. Acts 4:12 tells us, "There is none other name under heaven given among men, whereby we must be saved." "Thou shalt call his name Jesus: for he shall save his people from their sins" (Matt. 1:21). A name given from heaven. A name great in history. A name glorious in honor. A name gracious in help.

What do you need today? Jesus Christ can provide it in the will of God, if you will call on the name of Jesus, for "whosoever shall call on the name of the Lord shall be saved" (Acts 2:21). That name which is above every name is the name of Jesus.